THE MEANING O

by Jacques M

A REQUEST OF REVISION TO THE TRANSLATION OF 23 NEW TESTAMENT PASSAGES

Matthew 20:16; Matthew 22:14; Matthew 24:22;

Matthew 24:24; Matthew 24:31

Mark 13:20; Mark 13:22; Mark 13:27

Luke 18:7; Luke 23:35

Romans 8:33; Romans 16:13

Colossians 3:12

1 Timothy 5:21; 2 Timothy 2:10

Titus 1:1

1 Peter 1:2; 1 Peter 2:4; 1 Peter 2:6; 1 Peter 2:9

2 John 1; 2 John 13

Revelation 17:14

THE MEANING OF *eklektos*

by Jacques More

There are many places in the New Testament where the Greek word *eklektos* is found. It has been translated as 'chosen' (7) and 'elect' (16) in English (numbers reflect the frequency in the KJV). Such that the following verses include them and are well known:

> ...For many are called, but few chosen.
> *Matthew 20:16 & 22:14*

> But you *are* a chosen generation, a royal priesthood, a holy nation, His own special people...
> *1 Peter 2:9*

> I charge *you* before God and the Lord Jesus Christ and the elect angels...
> *1 Timothy 5:21*

> For false christs and false prophets will arise and...deceive, if possible, even the elect.
> *Matthew 24:24 & Mark 13:22*

> And He will send His angels...and they will gather together His elect from the four winds, from one end of heaven to the other.
> *Matthew 24:31 & Mark 13:27*

> Who shall bring a charge against God's elect?...
> *Romans 8:33*

I wish to bring evidence to light which shows these are inaccurate translations of *eklektos*. The writers of the New Testament used the Greek of the day as their language and, as shown by their quotes of the Old Testament, were well-versed in the language employed by the Greek Version of the Hebrew scripture. This is known as the Septuagint. This text reveals that *eklektos* to the common reader was understood as 'quality', 'special', 'choice' (in that sense), 'best', 'tops', etc. The flavour is one of quality and not a selection as has been understood by 'chosen' and 'elect'. This would make the above passages read like this:

> **...For many are called, but few are fit for it.**
> *Matthew 20:16 & 22:14* **JM**

> **But you are a quality generation, a royal priesthood, a holy nation, His own special people...**
> *1 Peter 2:9* **JM**

> **I charge you before God and the Lord Jesus Christ and the good angels...**
> *1 Timothy 5:21* **JM**

> **For false christs and false prophets will arise and... deceive, if possible, even the saints [the good guys].**
> *Matthew 24:24 & Mark 13:22* **JM**

> **And He will send His angels...and they will gather together His precious ones [the good guys] from the four winds, from one end of heaven to the other.**
> *Matthew 24:31 & Mark 13:27* **JM**

> **Who shall bring a charge against God's precious?...**
> *Romans 8:33* **JM**

Of course, quality being the emphasis a number of possible alternatives in English give the intended flavour. As long as the 'idea' of selection as implied is removed when quality is the reality then the translation becomes more accurate and true to the original meaning intended.

Evidence that the writers of the New Testament used the Septuagint

It is of note here that the inspiration of the Septuagint is not at issue here, but the use of the Greek language in which it was translated and this being known by the writers of the New Testament. When Alexander the Great conquered the whole Mediterranean region and then the various Greek dynasties ruled, Greek became the main language of communication between peoples and for commerce.

So that when the Romans then conquered the region Greek was very much in use. The Septuagint, with the reference LXX, is the Greek translation of the Hebrew Old Testament of the Bible. Tradition has it as translated by 70 scholars hence its name. It was carried out within the period of 285-247BC in Alexandria, Egypt and became the common used Bible for Jesus, the apostles and the first Christians.

This use by the apostles and Jesus can be seen by their quotes of the Old Testament

Away with you, Satan! For it is written, 'You shall worship the LORD your God, and Him only you shall serve.'
Matthew 4:10

The Septuagint contains the words 'kai autô monô'[1], in English 'and Him only', and this 'only' translated from Deuteronomy 6:13 is not found in the Hebrew. Which is why when the Old Testament quoted by Jesus and the other apostles are looked up in our Bibles these are not found. Our Old Testaments are translated direct from the Hebrew.

'These people draw near to Me with their mouth, and honor Me with their lips, but their heart is far from Me. And in vain they worship Me, teaching as doctrines the commandments of men.'
Matthew 15:8-9

This is a quote by Jesus primarily of Isaiah 29:13. Similar sentiments are found in Psalm 78:36 and Ezekiel 33:31. The Hebrew does not contain 'in vain they worship Me' whilst it is there in the Septuagint 'matên de debontai me'. This vouches therefore for Matthew and Jesus' use of the Septuagint. A good example of Paul's use of it:

Beloved, do not avenge yourselves, but *rather* give place to wrath; for it is written, 'Vengeance is Mine, I will repay,' says the Lord. 'Therefore if your enemy hungers, feed him; if he thirsts, give him a drink; for in so doing you will heap coals of fire on his head.'
Romans 12:19-20

This latter OT quote is direct from Proverbs 25:21-22. The Greek is exactly the same in the Septuagint to the New Testament Text. Whilst in the Hebrew Text and our Bibles Proverbs 25:21-22 reads,

If your enemy is hungry, give him bread to eat; and if he is thirsty, give him water to drink; for *so* you will heap coals of fire on his head...
Proverbs 25:21-22

Paul makes no mention of bread or water but it is clearly there in the Hebrew. Equally he mentions 'in so doing' which is in the Septuagint and nowhere in the Hebrew.

This use of the Septuagint makes it a valuable resource for appreciating the meaning of words in the language of the New Testament. If a word can be clearly shown to have an emphasis different than has up till now been used, then we should take notice. A revision of this translation would thereby be called upon. I believe this is the case for the word *eklektos*. It has been translated as 'chosen' and 'elect' giving an idea of a selection. Whilst the Greek writers used *hairetizô* as in Matthew 12:18 and *eklegô* as in Acts 15:22,25 for chosen in terms of selection.

The body of proof for *eklektos* as quality

All the places where it is found in the Septuagint are mentioned. These are compared to the English translation for the Hebrew word for which the Greek translator made use of *eklektos*. The regular and common use of it for quality is readily visible.

Here follows a full list[2] of references where the word **eklektos** is to be found in the Septuagint[3]:

KEY:
In **bold** are the translations of *eklektos* involving quality.
Underlined are the translations, as quoted, involving a decision, an alternative picked.

In borders are the translations of both types for the same Greek word.

COMMENT:
The amount of these (bordered) combined with the consistent **quality** emphasis show this as the normal 'feel' for the word *eklektos*.
The added fact that, there is no undisputed translation with the idea of chosen, elect-ed where an individual or group of people are not involved, makes one ask what honest criteria was used to do so where individuals and particular groups are mentioned?

REFERENCE		GREEK	A DIRECT TRANSLATIC
Genesis	23:6	tois eklektois	our **choice** sepulchres
	41:2	eklektai	seven cows...**choice** of flesh
	4	tas eklektas	**choice**-fleshed cows
	5	eklektoi	seven ears...**choice** and good
	7	tous eklektous	seven **choice** and full ears
	18	eklektai	**choice**-fleshed
	20	tas eklektas	**choice** cows
Exodus	14:7	eklekta	six hundred _chosen_ chariots
	30:23	eklektês	the flower of **choice** myrrh
Numbers	11:28	ho eklektos	Joshua...the _chosen_ one
Deuteronomy	12:11	eklekton	every **choice** gift of yours
Judges	20:15	eklektoi	seven hundred _chosen_ men
	34	eklektôn	ten thousand _chosen_ men
1 Samuel	24:3	eklektous	three thousand men _chosen_
(LXX: 1 Kings)	26:2	eklektoi	three thousand men _chosen_
2 Samuel	8:8	tôn eklektôn	the **choice** cities
(LXX: 2 Kings)	21:6	eklektous	_chosen_ out for the Lord [the men]
	22:27	eklektou	with the **excellent**...
	27	eklektos	...you will be **excellent**
1 Kings (3)p46_bis_		eklektoi	ten **choice** calves
(LXX: 3 Kings)	4:23	eklektoi	ten **choice** calves
	23	eklektôn	and **choice** fatted does
2 Kings	8:12	tous eklektous	their **choice** men
(LXX: 4 Kings)	19:23	ta eklekta	his **choice** cypresses
1 Chronicles	7:40	eklektoi	**choice**, mighty men
	9:22	hoi eklektoi	All the _chosen_ porters
	16:13	eklektoi	Jacob his _chosen ones_
	18:8	tôn eklektôn	out of **the chief** cities
Ezra	5:8	eklektois	with **choice** stones
Nehemiah	5:18	eklekta	six **choice** sheep
Job	37:11	eklekton	a cloud obscures [what is] **preciou**
Psalm	17:26	eklektou	with the **excellent**
	26	eklektos	thou wilt be **excellent**
	77:31	tous eklektous	the **choice** men
	88:3	tois eklektois	my _chosen_ ones
	19	eklekton	one _chosen_ out of .
	104:6	eklektoi	his _chosen ones_
	43	tous eklektous	his _chosen_

the *choice* of our...
*fat*fleshed
fat kine
rank and good
[rank: Eng. in the sense of complete] (Heb. *fat*.)
rank and full ears
*fat*fleshed
fat kine

---

*chosen[4] chariots
choice chariots **NKJV**; the *best* chariots **NIV**

---

pure myrrh

---

of his *young* men
of his *choice* men **NKJV**; assistant since *youth* **NIV**

---

your *choice* vows
(Heb. the *choice* of your vows.)

---

*chosen men
select men **NKJV**; *chosen* men **NIV**
*chosen men
select men **NKJV**; *finest* men **NIV**

24:2 **chosen* men
*chosen men
N/A
the LORD did *†choose*
(Or, *chosen* of the LORD.)
With the *pure...*
show thyself *pure*
N/A
Ten *fat* oxen
and *fatted* fowl
their *young* men
the *choice* fir trees
choice and mighty men
^chosen to be porters
his *†chosen ones*
N/A
with *great* stones
six *choice* sheep
N/A
18:26 With the *pure...*
18:26 show thyself *pure*

It is of note that some small sections of the LXX are not found in the hebrew scripture and therefore not in the Old Testament of our Bibles. Equally, it must be recognised that in places the translation into the Greek was 'loose' and not literal, such that when a direct counterpart in the Hebrew is non existent, the Hebrew translation into the English does not exist. These are 2 different reasons for which N/A has been placed in the KJV column.

78:31 *‡chosen* [men]
the *choice* [men] **NKJV**; the *young* men **NIV**; (Or, *young men* **KJV**)

89:3 my *†chosen*

89:19 **chosen* out of
one *chosen* from **NKJV**; a *young man* from **NIV**

105:6 his *†chosen*
105:43 his *†chosen*

REFERENCE		GREEK	A DIRECT TRANSLATIC
	105:5	tôn eklektôn	thine _elect_
	23	ho eklektos	his _chosen_
	140:4	tôn eklektôn	_their_ **choice ones**
Proverbs	8:19	eklektou	**choice** silver
	12:24	eklektôn	_chosen_ men
	17:3	eklektai	**choice** hearts
Cant.	5:15	eklektos	**choice** as the cedars
	6:8	eklektê	the **choice** of her
	9	eklektê	**choice** as the sun
Isaiah	22:7	hai eklektai	**thy choice** valleys
	8	tous eklektous	**the choice** houses
	28:16	eklekton	a costly stone, a **choice**
	40:30	eklektoi	the **choice** [men]
	42:1	ho eklektos	Israel is my _chosen_
	43:20	to eklekton	to my _chosen_
	45:4	tou eklektou	Israel mine _elect_
	49:2	eklekton	a **choice** shaft
	54:12	eklektous	**precious** stones
	65:9	hoi eklektoi	mine _elect_, and my servants
	15	tois eklektois	my _chosen_
	23	hoi eklektoi	My _chosen_
Jeremiah	3:19	eklektên	a **choice** land
	10:17	eklektois	**choice** [vessels]
	22:7	tas eklektas	**thy choice** cedars
	26:15	ho eklektos	**thy choice** calf
	31:15	eklektoi	his **choice** young men
	38:39	eklektôn	**choice** stones
Lamentations	1:15	eklektous	my **choice** men
	5:13	eklektoi	the _chosen_ men
	14	eklektoi	the _chosen_ men
Ezekiel	7:20	eklekta	their **choice** ornaments
	17:22	tôn eklektôn	of the **choice** [branches] of the ced
	19:12	ta eklekta	her **choice** [branches]
	14	eklektôn	her **choice** [boughs]
	25:9	eklektên	the **choice** land
	27:20	eklektôn	**choice** cattle
	24	eklektous	**choice** stores
	31:16	ta eklekta	the **choice** [plants]
Daniel	11:15	hoi eklektoi	his _chosen_ ones
Amos	5:11	eklekta	**choice** gifts
Habakkuk	1:16	eklekta	meats **choice**
Haggai	2:7	ta eklekta	**the choice** [portions]
Zechariah	7:14	eklektên	the **choice** land
	11:16	tôn eklektôn	the flesh of **the choice [ones]**

KJV (from the Hebrew)

106:5 thy _tchosen_
106:23 his _tchosen_
141:4 their **dainties**
choice silver

> the **diligent** (= NKJV = NIV)

N/A
*__excellent__ as the cedars
6:9 the **choice [one]** of her
6:10 _clear_ as the sun
thy choicest valleys
the armour of the house
a **tried** stone
the **young** men
mine _telect_
my _tchosen_
Israel mine _telect_
a **polished** shaft
pleasant stones
mine _telect_
my _tchosen_
65:22 mine _telect_
a **pleasant** land
(Heb. land of **desire**)
N/A
thy **choice** cedars
46:15 thy valiant [men]

> **48:15** his _°chosen_ young
> (Heb. the **choice of**....)

N/A
my **young** men

> the **young** men
> the **young** men

the **beauty** of his ornaments
of the **highest** branch
her **fruit**
her **fruit**
the **glory** of the country
precious clothes
(Heb. clothes of **freedom**)
chests of **rich** apparel
the **choice** and best

> his _°chosen_ people
> his **choice** troops NKJV; their **best** troops NIV; (Heb. the people of his _choices_)

burdens of wheat
meat **plenteous**
(Or, **dainty**) Heb. **fat**
the **desire** of all nations
the **pleasant** land
eat the flesh of **the fat**

Robert Young author of the *Analitical Concordance to the Bible* makes a valuable comment. In *his research involving the useage of every word of Greek and Hebrew used in the Bible* he more than most can testify to the reality of what **eklektos** stood for. In the introduction to the New Testament of his Literal Version[5] of the Bible, he has listed what should be read in place of certain words. He lists a minimum of 100 words with a return to the original intent alongside.

| For <u>chosen</u> he has put: | read **choice one,** | very often in N.T. |
| For <u>elect</u>: | read **choice one,** | very often in S.S |

Basic analysis:

There are 82 occasions where the word *eklektos* is found in the Septuagint. Of these 7 have no corresponding section of writing in the Hebrew scripture as found translated in the Old Testament. This leaves us with 75 places where the word is found.

Out of 75 places 23 have been translated from the Hebrew into the KJV as follows: *chosen* (18); *elect* (4); *choose* (1).

This leaves us with 52 places where the translation (in the KJV) from the Hebrew words associated with *eklektos* are as follows:

choice (9); young [men] (6); pure (5); fat (4); pleasant (3);
rank [eng. complete] (2); fruit (2); fatfleshed (2);
highest [branch] (1); fatted (1); great [stones] (1);
diligent (1); excellent (1); clear [as the sun] (1);
thy choicest [valley] (1); the armour [of the house] (1);
tried [stone] (1); polished [shaft] (1); beauty (1); glory (1);
precious [clothes] (1); rich [apparel] (1);
burdens [of wheat] (1); plenteous (or, dainty) [meat] (1);
the desire [of all nations] (1); valiant (1); dainties (1).

It is undisputed therefore that the Greek thinkers who put together the Septuagint saw the understanding of quality as the prominent flavour for the word *eklektos*.

As mentioned above there are however 18 places (in the KJV) where *chosen* is found, 4 with *elect* and 1 with *choose* from Hebrew words associated with *eklektos*. The references for these are as follows:

chosen: Exodus 14:7**; Judges 20:15**; Judges 20:34**; 1 Samuel 24:3; 1 Samuel 26:2; 1 Chronicles 9:22; 1 Chronicles 16:13; Psalm 77:31**; Psalm 88:3; Psalm 88:19**; Psalm 104:6; Psalm 104:43; Psalm 105:5; Psalm 105:23; Isaiah 43:20; Isaiah 65:15; Jeremiah 31:15**; Daniel 11:15**

elect: Isaiah 42:1; Isaiah 45:4; Isaiah 65:9; Isaiah 65:23

choose: 2 Samuel 21:6

I have marked 7 of the references with a double star because they are translated differently in the margin of the KJV or other versions like the NKJV or NIV as follows:

Exodus 14:7	*choice* chariots **NKJV;**	the *best* chariots **NIV**
Judges 20:15	*select* men **NKJV;**	*chosen* men **NIV**
Judges 20:34	*select* men **NKJV;**	*finest* men **NIV**
Psalm 77:31	the *choice* [men] **NKJV;**	the *young* men **NIV;** (Or, *young men* **KJV**)
Psalm 88:19	one *chosen* from **NKJV;**	a *young* man **NIV**
Jeremiah 31:15 (48:15 in our Bibles)	**AV** margin: Heb. the *choice* of...	
Daniel 11:15	his *choice* troops **NKJV;**	their *best* troops **NIV**

This means that 7 can reasonably be removed from the list as meaning *chosen* and added to the one where *quality* is the prime emphasis. There is doubt of a 'selection' being the only emphasis.

New tally: - quality (type) 59 - chosen 11 - elect 4 - choose 1 -

The 'selection' words can be looked at with reference to the Hebrew words from which they are translated:

*BACHAR   chosen (2); [excellent (1)]

†BACHIR   chosen (8); elect (4); choose (1)

^BARAR   chosen (1)

Not only is BACHAR translated as 'excellent' in Song of Solomon 5:15, it is found translated in the LXX without reference to *eklektos*, as 'young men' in 2 Samuel 6:1, 1 Kings 12:21, 2 Chronicles 11:1 and Jeremiah 29:19 (49:19). As 'mighty warriors' in 2 Chronicles 13:3 and 13:17. As 'mighty men' in 2 Chronicles 13:17. As 'youths' in Jeremiah 27:44 (50:44). This of course brings doubt on the 'selection' emphasis.

New tally: - quality (type) 61 - chosen 9 - elect 4 - choose 1 -

---

BARAR is found in the KJV variously in regards to its root meaning of 'to clarify', 'to examine' or, 'test'. It is found with a 'quality' emphasis in words like 'choice' (2): 1 Chronicles 7:40; Nehemiah 5:18, 'polished' (1): Isaiah 49:2, 'pure' (1): Zephaniah 3:9, et al. Thus anything 'chosen' is due to its quality being discovered (after a testing).

This automatically gives us a new tally:
            - quality (type) 62 - chosen 8 - elect 4 - choose 1 -

The remainder is translated from BACHIR.
Could it be the Septuagint translators felt that BACHIR in the context they found it was understandable as 'quality' and thus used *eklektos*?

Conclusion:

Suffice to say that in the 1st century a reader of the New Testament had knowledge of the Greek as found in the Septuagint. Seeing as this Old Testament Version had the fat cows that came out of the Nile in Pharaoh's dream which Joseph interpreted as *eklektos* cows. And that quality silver is *eklektos* silver. And young men (guys in their prime) are known as *eklektos*. When he read in Matthew that Jesus said 'Many are called, few *eklektos*' he fully understood that few were quality and fit for that calling.

NOTES:

1 In Greek there are 2 'o's as letters. (O) omicron and (ω) omega. I denote omicron with an ordinary 'o' and omega with 'ô'. Similarly there is (ε) epsilon and (η) eta. I denote epsilon with an ordinary 'e' and eta with 'ê'.

2 The initial list worked from was taken from *A CONCORDANCE OF THE SEPTUAGINT* compiled by George Morrish and published by Zondervan. First published in 1887.

3 Both Greek words and the initial translation quoted are taken from *THE SEPTUAGINT WITH APOCRYPHA: GREEK AND ENGLISH* by Sir Lancelot C.L. Brenton and published by Hendrikson. Originally published in 1851.

4 The following symbols have been used to identify which Hebrew word *'chosen'*, *'elect'*, *'choose'* and *'excellent'* were translated from: *bachar; †bachir; ‡bachur; ^barar; °mibchar.

5 *YOUNG'S literal translation of the HOLY BIBLE* by Robert Young, Revised Edition published by Baker Book House. Third Edition January 1898.